NATIONAL GEOGRAPHIC KiDS

weird but true! 6

350 OUTRAGEOUS FACTS

NATIONAL GEOGRAPHIC
WASHINGTON, D.C.

SCIENTISTS USED SATELLITE IMAGES TO COUNT EMPEROR PENGUINS FROM SPACE.

THE **ASIAN WEAVER ANT** CAN HOLD OBJECTS **100 TIMES** ITS WEIGHT— WHILE HANGING **UPSIDE DOWN!**

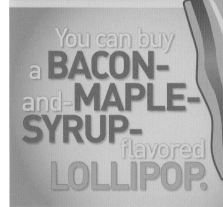

You can buy a **BACON-and-MAPLE-SYRUP-**flavored **LOLLIPOP.**

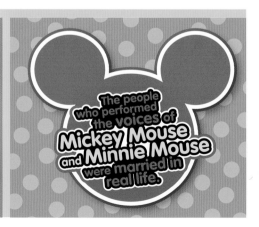

The people who performed the voices of **Mickey Mouse** and **Minnie Mouse** were married in real life.

A STUDY FOUND THAT
HOT CHOCOLATE
TASTES SWEETER
WHEN YOU DRINK IT FROM

AN
ORANGE
CUP
VS.
A
WHITE
CUP.

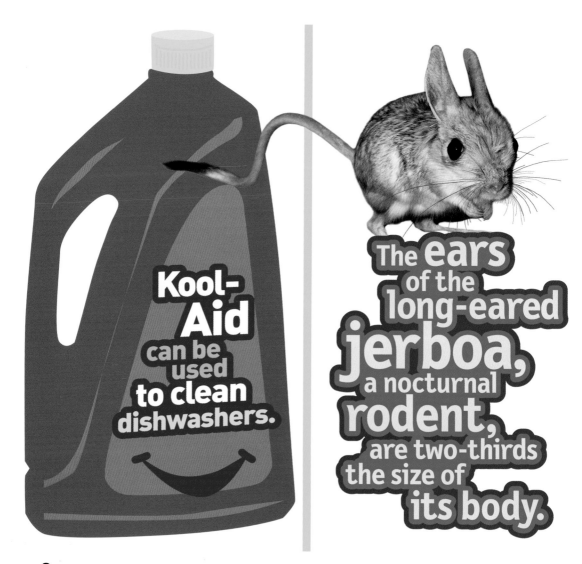

Kool-Aid can be used **to clean** dishwashers.

The **ears** of the **long-eared jerboa,** a nocturnal **rodent,** are two-thirds the size of **its body.**

8

THERE'S A FUNGUS THAT SECRETES RED DROPS THAT LOOK LIKE BLOOD.

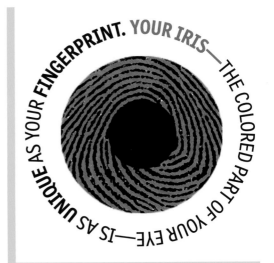

YOUR IRIS—THE COLORED PART OF YOUR EYE—IS AS UNIQUE AS YOUR FINGERPRINT.

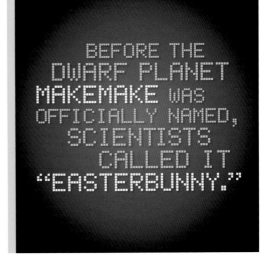

BEFORE THE DWARF PLANET MAKEMAKE WAS OFFICIALLY NAMED, SCIENTISTS CALLED IT "EASTERBUNNY."

PANDAS eat

AS MUCH AS

80 pounds
OF (36 kg)

bamboo
every
day—

THAT'S AS HEAVY AS

320 hamburgers!

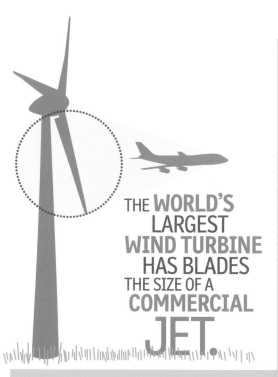

THE **WORLD'S** LARGEST **WIND TURBINE** HAS BLADES THE SIZE OF A **COMMERCIAL JET.**

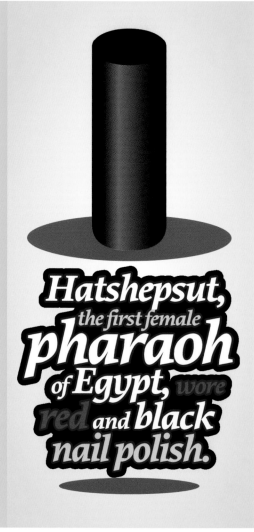

Hatshepsut, the first female **pharaoh** *of Egypt, wore red and black nail polish.*

SOME ANCIENT ROMANS RUBBED **CROCODILE DUNG** ON THEIR FACES TO BRIGHTEN THEIR SKIN.

A group of flamingos is called a flamboyance.

For 213 years it was **illegal for women to wear pants in Paris—** luckily the law was never really enforced.

You will almost never see a full moon and the sun in the sky at the same time.

THE JUICE OF **ONE** TYPE OF **CHILI PEPPER** CAN **BURN** THROUGH A **LATEX GLOVE.**

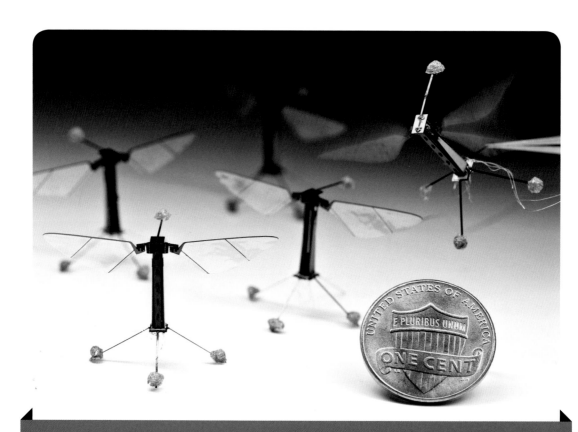

A FLYING ROBOT
CALLED ROBOBEE
IS ONLY SLIGHTLY LARGER THAN A PENNY.

1.9 BILLION YEARS AGO, MUCH OF THE EARTH SMELLED LIKE ROTTEN EGGS.

The Goliath spider's fangs are as long as a paper clip.

THE SHINIEST LIVING THING ON EARTH IS AN AFRICAN FRUIT KNOWN AS *POLLIA CONDENSATA*.

Male blue-footed **boobies** do a **high-step strut** to attract mates.

A **planet** partially made of **diamond** was calculated to be worth **$26.9 nonillion** (that's 26.9 plus 29 zeros)!

FOR
$100,000,
YOU CAN BUY A
KILLER WHALE–
SHAPED
SUBMARINE.

Humans could **LAUGH** before they could **TALK.**

A MASS OF **FLOATING ICE** THAT LOOKS LIKE AN **ICEBERG** IS CALLED A **FLOEBERG.**

IF YOU **ROLLED ALL THE WATER ON EARTH INTO A BALL,** IT WOULD BE LESS THAN A THIRD THE SIZE OF THE MOON.

EARTH

MOON

WATER ON EARTH

Indian **giant squirrels** can leap up to **20 feet** (6 m) — about as long as a giraffe is tall.

SOME DOGS ARE ALLERGIC TO CATS.

**The world's largest
toilet-paper pyramid
was made up of
23,821 rolls.**

THE HAGFISH IS THE ONLY ANIMAL THAT HAS A SKULL BUT NO SPINE.

A PET **RABBIT** IN ENGLAND **WEIGHS** THE SAME AS **FOUR** BOWLING BALLS.

A WOMAN ONCE DISLOCATED HER JAW WHILE EATING A **GIANT** HAMBURGER.

Sunlight **reflected** off a **building in** London, England, **melted** a nearby car.

Saturn's moon PAN
IS SHAPED LIKE A WALNUT.

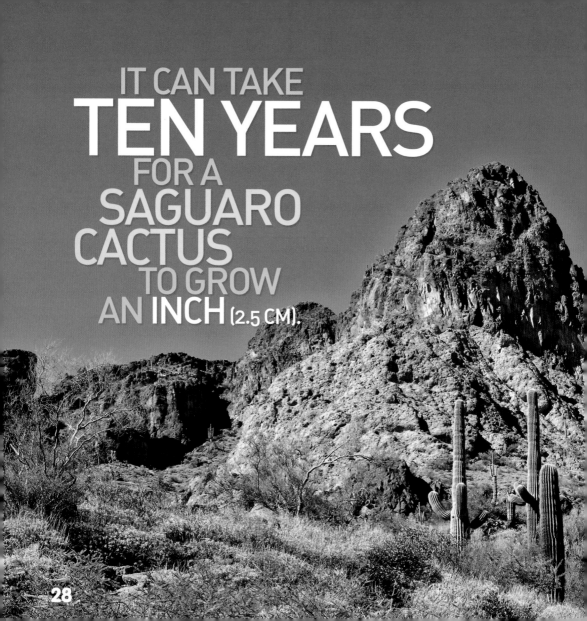

IT CAN TAKE **TEN YEARS** FOR A SAGUARO CACTUS TO GROW AN **INCH** (2.5 CM).

A chunk of **rock** about as long as **17,000 basketball courts** was seen floating in the South Pacific.

Ghost ants have SEE-THROUGH STOMACHS.

A PIECE OF **CAKE** FROM **QUEEN VICTORIA'S** *wedding* HAS BEEN PRESERVED IN **ENGLAND** SINCE 1840.

A company invented a **remote-controlled helicopter** that's the size of a **golf ball.**

KOMODO DRAGONS OFTEN VOMIT WHEN THREATENED.

SOME PLANTS **GLOW** BRIGHT BLUE UNDER ULTRAVIOLET LIGHT.

MORE THAN
HALF
THE
WORLD'S
GEYSERS
ARE IN
YELLOWSTONE
NATIONAL
PARK
IN WYOMING, U.S.A.

THE NIGHT SIDE OF PLANET EARTH IS 600,000 TIMES DIMMER THAN ITS DAY SIDE.

The largest **kangaroos** can weigh as much as **grown men.**

NASA IS DEVELOPING A **3-D PRINTER** THAT IT HOPES WILL "PRINT" **EDIBLE** PIZZAS.

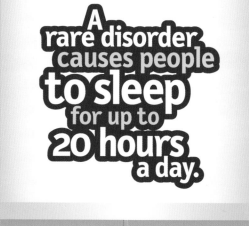

A **rare disorder** causes people **to sleep** for up to **20 hours** a day.

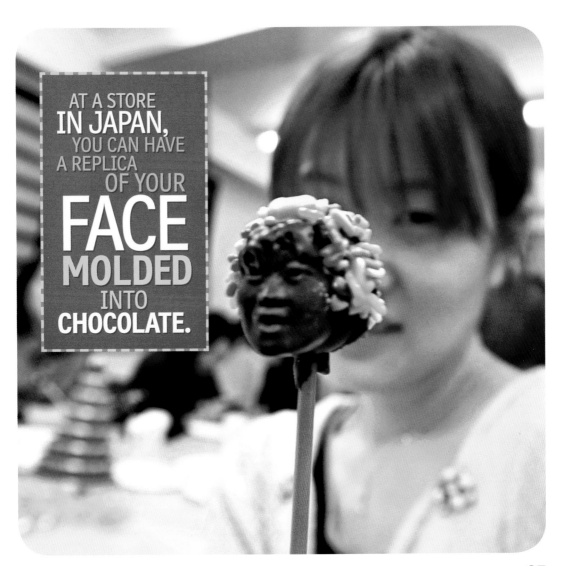

AT A STORE **IN JAPAN,** YOU CAN HAVE A REPLICA OF YOUR **FACE** MOLDED INTO **CHOCOLATE.**

The **bee hummingbird** snacks on up to **1,500 flowers a day.**

A SCULPTOR CARVED A **LIFE-SIZE ASTRONAUT** FROM A **ONE-TON** (0.9-t) **BLOCK OF CHEDDAR CHEESE.**

AN ASTRONAUT WROTE HIS DAUGHTER'S INITIALS ON THE DUSTY SURFACE OF THE MOON.

Some frogs eat crabs.

FOSSILS OF EARTH'S EARLIEST KNOWN ANIMALS

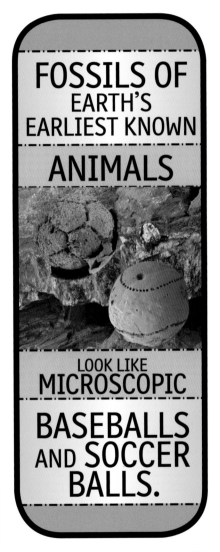

LOOK LIKE MICROSCOPIC BASEBALLS AND SOCCER BALLS.

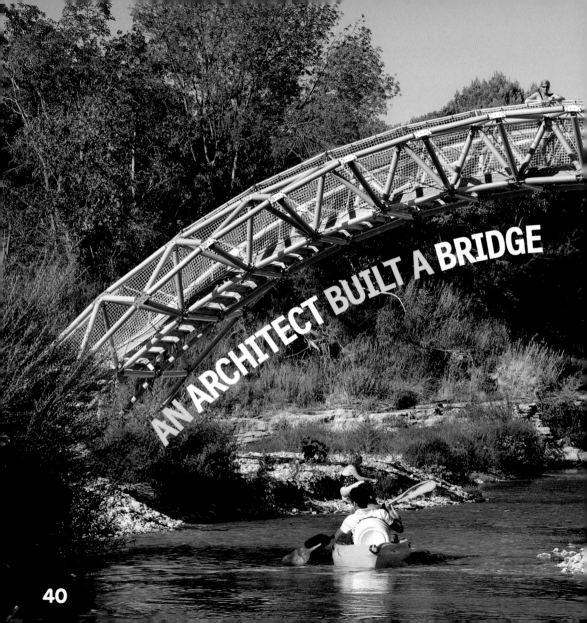

AN ARCHITECT BUILT A BRIDGE

OUT OF CARDBOARD TUBES.

THE **PIRATE ANT** IS NAMED FOR THE **BLACK PATCHES** ON ITS EYES.

Some **catfish** **leap** out of the **water** to **catch pigeons** on the shore.

Female **fireflies** rarely **fly.**

Americans **eat** over a **billion chicken wings** during **Super Bowl** weekend.

People **throw away** *enough* **ribbon** *each year to* **tie a bow** *around the entire* **Earth.**

About **one** out of **five people** have dropped their cell phone into the **toilet.**

A train track in Chongqing, China, runs through the middle of a **19-STORY APARTMENT BUILDING.**

The best way to treat a **JELLYFISH STING** is to put **VINEGAR** on it.

Exoplanet KELT-11b would float in water.

The substance that mussels use to attach themselves to rocks can **HELP WOUNDS HEAL WITHOUT SCARRING.**

Researchers created an **"OSTRICH ROBOT"** that can run on **TWO LEGS.**

Scientists have genetically engineered microbes to **"SEE" COLOR.**

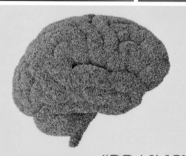

PLANTS HAVE "BRAINS" THAT DECIDE WHEN THE PLANTS GROW.

ANCIENT SEA SCORPIONS may have used their **SPIKED TAILS** TO SLASH PREY.

The **DUST ON MARS** and the moon could someday be used to print 3-D objects such as tools for missions.

The skin on the soles of astronauts' feet peels off during long space missions.

BEIBEILONG SINENSIS was a dinosaur that **LAID EGGS** up to **TWO FEET** (0.6 m) long.

Researchers invented a **DEVICE** that can turn **AIR POLLUTION INTO FUEL.**

That's Weird!

LADYBUGS
raise their shells and **unfold their wings from underneath** like origami, one study found.

A LEGO SCULPTURE OF ENGLAND'S QUEEN ELIZABETH II INCLUDED A CROWN WITH REAL DIAMONDS.

Borborygmus

is the word for the **rumbling sound** in your **stomach** when you're **hungry.**

Louis XIV of *France* wore *four-inch-high heels.* (10-cm)

The gray **catbird** makes a **meow** sound.

200 million Girl Scout **cookies** are sold every year— enough for each person in the U.S. to have half a box.

Some **green snakes** turn **blue** when they **die.**

47

A **GORILLA** AT A **ZOO** IN **GERMANY** CAN **WALK** ON A **TIGHT-ROPE.**

49

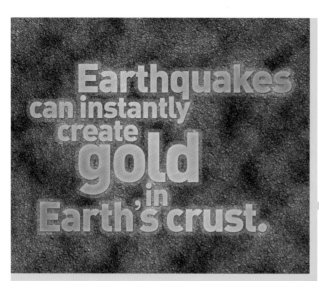

Earthquakes can instantly create **gold** in Earth's crust.

An **avocado** is sometimes known as an **alligator pear.**

More people hide their **valuables** in their **sock drawer** than anywhere else, according to a British study.

A **SIX-CLAWED** LOBSTER WAS CAUGHT OFF THE COAST OF **MASSACHUSETTS,** U.S.A.

Wild strawberries can be yellow.

THERE'S A TOWN IN CANADA CALLED SAINT-LOUIS-DU-HA! HA!

A WOOD FROG'S CROAK SOUNDS LIKE A QUACK.

SOME GRASSHOPPERS ARE PINK.

Scientists found that you can literally get **cold feet** when you're nervous.

IN ANCIENT GREECE, COMETS WERE CALLED "HAIRY STARS."

Some **house ants** smell like **fresh coconuts** when *smashed.*

BUT *DON'T GO AROUND* SMASHING ANTS, PLEASE!

A woman in Sweden found her **wedding ring** on a **carrot** growing in her garden—16 years after misplacing it!

53

30 feet (9.1 m)

SUNFLOWERS CAN GROW TALLER THAN TWO AFRICAN ELEPHANTS STACKED UP.

The movie *Cloudy With a Chance of Meatballs* is called *Rain of Falafel* in Israel.

IN THE WILD, **GOLDFISH** CAN GROW TO BE MORE THAN A **FOOT LONG.**
(0.3 m)

Your palm will **NEVER** become as **TAN** as the **TOP** of **your HAND.**

Locusts are a **popular snack** in parts of **Africa** and **Asia.**

SCANDINAVIANS IN NORWAY TRAVELED ON HANDMADE SKIS MORE THAN 8,000 YEARS AGO.

SCIENTISTS THINK THAT WATER ON THE MOON CAME FROM EARTH.

There's a road in New Jersey, U.S.A., named "Shades of Death."

57

A CYCLIST INVENTED A BIKE HELMET MADE FROM **RECYCLED NEWSPAPERS.**

AFRICAN LIONS
CATCH ABOUT
25 PERCENT
OF THE PREY
THEY CHASE.

25%

DRAGONFLIES
CATCH
95 PERCENT.

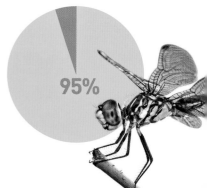

95%

A 10-YEAR-OLD KID IS MADE UP OF ABOUT 3,200,000,000,000,000,000,000,000,000 ATOMS.

59

A WILD
BEAR
IN TENNESSEE,
U.S.A.,
TRIED TO BREAK
INTO
A ZOO.

BEARS do not go to the **BATHROOM** for months while they're **HIBERNATING.**

THERE IS ABOUT
ONE BEAR FOR
EVERY
TWO PEOPLE
IN THE
YUKON TERRITORY, CANADA.

A GRIZZLY BEAR CAN SNIFF OUT FOOD 18 MILES (29 km) AWAY.

Electric taxis cruised the streets of New York City **more than 100** years ago.

New Zealand has more cats per person than any other country in the world.

A JAPANESE ARTIST MAKES **SHELLS** FOR **HERMIT CRABS** THAT LOOK LIKE **CITY SKYLINES.**

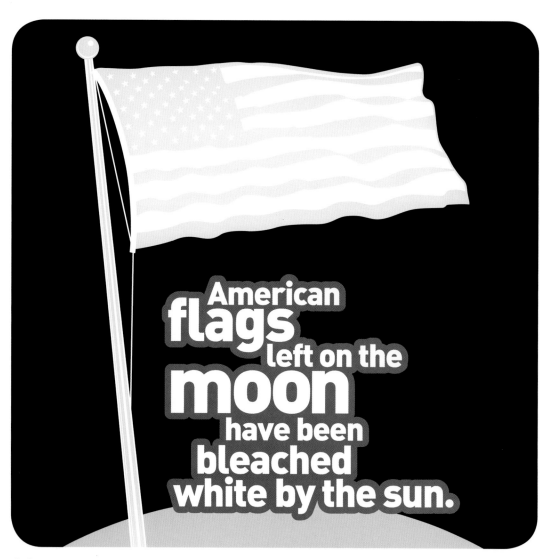

American **flags** left on the **moon** have been **bleached white by the sun.**

A *designer* created a **glow-in-the-dark** *wedding* *dress.*

T HOG WORLD

gammon and chicken sorbet
ith a crunchy canine biscuit
served in a cone.

E COOKIE CRUNCH

us doggie delight of mixed dog
and ice cream topped with a
one. Served in a traditional ice
one.

ree to donate 99p

AN **ICE-CREAM TRUCK** IN LONDON SERVED **SCOOPS** JUST FOR **DOGS.**

IT DOESN'T RAIN IN THE EYE OF A HURRICANE

A turtle's shell is made up of about 50 bones.

It is impossible to **hum** while holding **your nose.**

Atlantic lobsters sometimes **eat** each other.

A PICTURE PAINTED BY A RETIRED
RACEHORSE SOLD
FOR MORE THAN $2,000 on eBay.

A PALM TREE is not a tree; it's a type of GRASS.

NASCAR DRIVERS CAN TRAVEL THE **LENGTH**

OF A **FOOTBALL FIELD** IN JUST OVER A **SECOND.**

Some early **baseballs** were made of **fish eyes** covered in **leather.**

An **ELEPHANT'S skin** is as thick as **12 stacked PENNIES.**

A STUDY FOUND THAT **CHEESE** MAY TASTE **SALTIER** IF YOU **EAT** IT OFF A **KNIFE** INSTEAD OF A **FORK.**

STICK TO A FORK. IT'S SAFER!

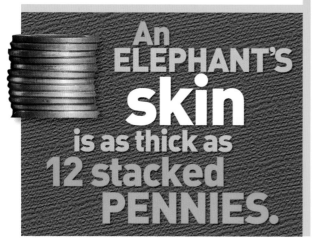

SEAGULLS
SOMETIMES SIT ON
PELICANS' HEADS.

The White House,
in Washington, D.C., U.S.A.,

was originally called the President's Palace.

A luxury **hotel** distributes 24-karat-gold **iPads** to its guests in Dubai, United Arab Emirates.

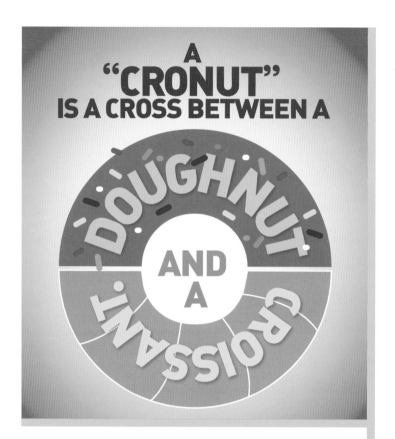

A "CRONUT" IS A CROSS BETWEEN A DOUGHNUT AND A CROISSANT.

Amazon.com was **originally called** "**CADABRA.**"

CHiMPANZEES CAN SWIM THE *BREASTSTROKE.*

AN EMU'S BODY CONTAINS UP TO THREE GALLONS OF OIL— (11.4 L) ENOUGH TO FILL THREE MILK JUGS.

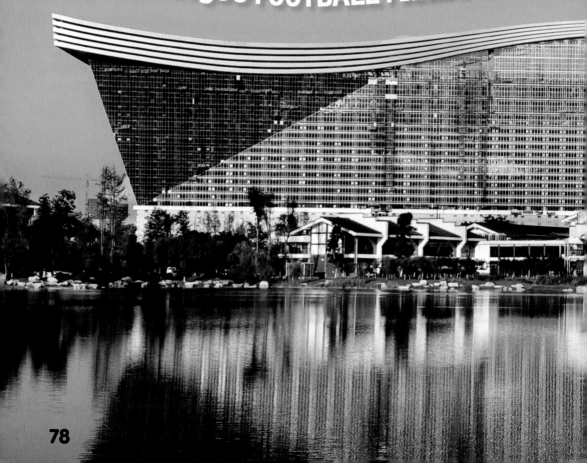

MORE THAN 300 FOOTBALL FIELDS COULD FIT

INTO THE **WORLD'S LARGEST BUILDING,** LOCATED IN CHINA.

Muscles make up about **half** your body weight.

The **COOKIECUTTER SHARK** is named for the **COOKIE-SHAPED WOUNDS** it leaves in its **PREY.**

YOU CAN BUY **CANDY** THAT YOU CAN DRINK FROM A MINI– **TOILET BOWL.**

STEP ONE: POUR IN CANDY

STEP TWO: STIR

STEP THREE: DRINK!

Giant kelp can grow up to **two feet** in a day. (0.6 m)

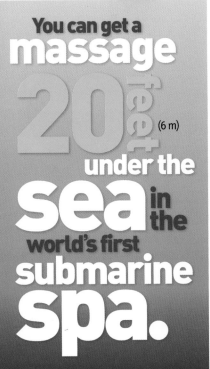

You can get a **massage** **20** feet (6 m) **under the** **sea** in the world's first **submarine** **spa.**

YOU LOSE ABOUT 500 **MILLION SKIN CELLS** EVERY **24 HOURS.**

The first ever webcam was used to watch a pot of coffee.

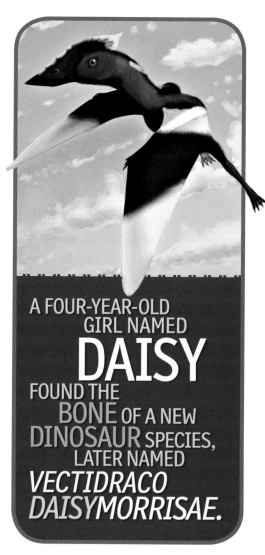

A FOUR-YEAR-OLD GIRL NAMED **DAISY** FOUND THE BONE OF A NEW DINOSAUR SPECIES, LATER NAMED *VECTIDRACO DAISYMORRISAE.*

Nosewise, Sturdy, and **Hardy** *were popular names* for dogs *in medieval times.*

SOME MOTHS' HEARING IS **150 TIMES MORE SENSITIVE** THAN A HUMAN'S.

DOCTORS IN BRAZIL ARE EXPERIMENTING WITH USING FISH SKIN AS BANDAGES FOR BURNS.

FUNGI LIVING IN A TOXIC LAKE WERE **FOUND TO PRODUCE A NEW** antibiotic.

The WORLD RECORD for the MOST SPOONS BALANCED on the HUMAN BODY is 50.

LIONFISH MAKE NOISES THAT SOUND LIKE **TINY DRUMBEATS.**

EGYPTIAN VULTURES USE RED MUD AS **"MAKEUP"** TO COLOR THEIR **FACES** AND **WHITE FEATHERS.**

A LIBRARIAN in Massachusetts, U.S.A., found live Civil War–era **MILITARY SHELLS** in her new office's **CLOSET.**

Some farmers use **"HAIL CANNONS"** to try to protect their crops from hailstorms.

THE KING of ENGLAND once had a **"GROOM OF THE STOOL,"** whose job was to **KEEP HIS MAJESTY COMPANY** while he used the toilet.

A **JAPANESE ARTIST** MAKES **BIRDS, SHRIMP,** AND **OTHER DESIGNS** OUT OF **WHOLE CITRUS PEELS.**

DRAGON SKIN ICE = **SEAWATER THAT FREEZES IN MIDAIR**

A VILLAGE in INDONESIA has hundreds of houses **PAINTED IN RAINBOW COLORS.**

A CANADIAN MAN INVENTED A **HOVERBOARD THAT CAN REACH 10,000 FEET** (3,045 M)—THAT'S ABOUT HALF THE HEIGHT OF MOUNT KILIMANJARO!

T. REX COULD BITE WITH **8,000 POUNDS** (3,630 KG) OF FORCE—THE EQUIVALENT OF BEING CRUSHED BY **THREE STACKED CARS.**

That's Weird!

A **DRAWING** BY LEONARDO DA VINCI— A FAMOUS 15TH-CENTURY ARTIST AND INVENTOR— INSPIRED THE DESIGN OF BATMAN'S **CAPE.**

MUSICIANS RE-CREATED THE **BATMAN** THEME SONG USING REAL BAT SOUNDS.

 THERE'S AN AIRPORT IN TURKEY NAMED BATMAN.

THE ORIGINAL **BATMOBILE** FROM THE **1960s** *BATMAN* TV SHOW SOLD FOR **$4.2 MILLION.**

SOME **FISH** USE THEIR **FINS TO WALK** ALONG THE **OCEAN FLOOR.**

The world's largest **AIRPLANE** could carry the weight of more than **160 hippos.**

Pac-Man's shape was inspired by a whole pizza with a slice removed.

BALD PEOPLE ACTUALLY HAVE MICROSCOPIC HAIRS ON THEIR **HEADS.**

You can tell the age of a **dolphin** by counting the layers within its **teeth**— like tree rings!

DOLPHINS CAN RECOGNIZE AN OLD FRIEND'S WHISTLE, EVEN AFTER THEY'VE BEEN SEPARATED FOR 20 YEARS.

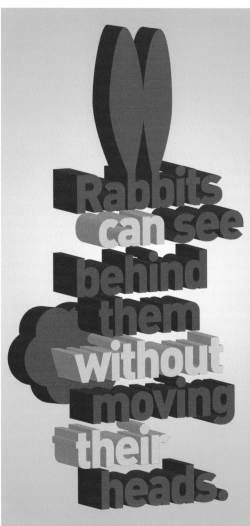

Rabbits can see behind them without moving their heads.

THERE'S A MONUMENT DEDICATED TO THE **BOLL WEEVIL BUG** IN ALABAMA, U.S.A.

94

AILUROPHOBIA IS AN EXTREME FEAR OF CATS.

Geckos communicate by barking, chirping, and squeaking.

Shrimp swim BACKWARD.

Three out of four people admitted to sharing an ice-cream cone **with their pet,** a survey found.

Flatworms can **regrow** their heads.

More than **200 million emails** are sent **every minute** *on Earth.*

A **PRISON** IN **BRAZIL** **USES GEESE** AS AN ALARM SYSTEM— THEY HONK AT ANYONE ROAMING THE GROUNDS!

99

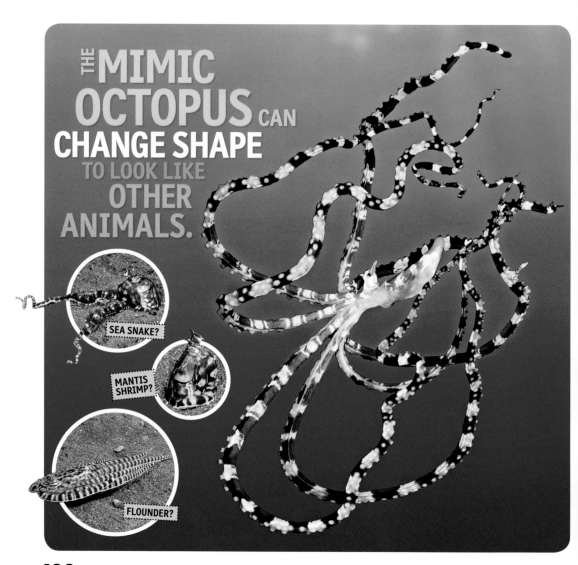

THE **MIMIC OCTOPUS** CAN **CHANGE SHAPE** TO LOOK LIKE **OTHER ANIMALS.**

SEA SNAKE?

MANTIS SHRIMP?

FLOUNDER?

THE INTERNATIONAL

SPACE STATION

IS THE MOST

EXPENSIVE

OBJECT EVER CONSTRUCTED— COSTING SOME

$130 BILLION TO BUILD.

HUNDREDS OF YEARS AGO,

RUSSIANS

BUILT THE FIRST

ROLLER COASTERS

FROM

ICE.

The world's fastest runner

generates enough energy in a 100-meter (328-foot) sprint **to power a vacuum.**

There's a **frog** that hears through its **mouth.**

THAT'S WEIRD!

Families in COLONIAL AMERICA

 sometimes ate popcorn like breakfast cereal (with cream and sugar!).

You have **taste buds** in your **throat.**

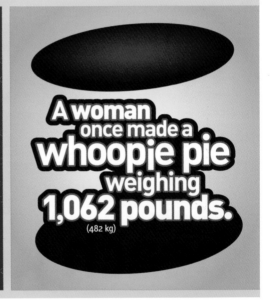

A woman once made a **whoopie pie** weighing **1,062 pounds.** (482 kg)

BAKED CATERPILLARS TASTE LIKE PISTACHIOS.

DON'T TRY THIS AT HOME!

The
blue whale—
the largest animal
on Earth—can't
swallow anything
bigger than a
beach ball.

BLUE WHALES DO UNDERWATER BARREL ROLLS BEFORE CATCHING PREY.

FOR THE FIRST SEVEN MONTHS OF THEIR LIVES.

STUDIES SHOW THAT THE AVERAGE DAYDREAM IS ABOUT 14 SECONDS LONG.

Male pandas sometimes do handstands to mark trees.

For $25, you can order a **jar of human toenails online.**

THE SPEED OF LIGHT IS 18 MILLION TIMES FASTER THAN THE SPEED OF RAIN.

*The **Kilauea volcano**, on the Big Island of Hawaii, U.S.A., has been erupting for more than **35 years.***

Before it hit stores, **the iPhone** was known as **"Purple."**

SOME **BIRDS** HIBERNATE.

ORANGUTANS
SOMETIMES MAKE
WHISTLES
OUT OF LEAVES.

NEARLY HALF THE WORLD'S LAND IS STILL WILDERNESS.

100 billion servings of **instant ramen noodles** are **sold every year.**

EVERY YEAR, RESIDENTS IN A NEW MEXICO, U.S.A., TOWN **BUILD A GIANT SNOWMAN** OUT OF **TUMBLEWEEDS.**

The longest unbroken apple peel was as long as an Olympic-size pool.

Bus-size **BLOBS** of grease, called **fatbergs,** can **clog** underground sewers.

A restaurant in Singapore once sold a **pizza within a pizza.**

Some **beetles' bellies glow** orange.

When threatened, a copperhead snake releases musk that smells like **cucumbers.**

STORM SYSTEMS IN THE SKY CAN HOLD **MORE WATER** THAN THE **MISSISSIPPI RIVER.**

IT TOOK **ARTISTS** SOME **17,000 HOURS** TO BUILD A **LIFE-SIZE STAR WARS X-WING STARFIGHTER** FROM **LEGO BRICKS.**

THE FURRY CHEWBACCA BAT IS NAMED AFTER THE **STAR WARS CHARACTER.**

A FAST FOOD RESTAURANT IN FRANCE OFFERED DARTH VADER **BURGERS WITH BUNS** THAT WERE DYED BLACK.

Perfectly preserved honey has been found in ancient Egyptian tombs.

You can order deep-fried jelly beans at some state fairs.

IT WOULD TAKE **225 MILLION YEARS TO WALK** A LIGHT-YEAR.

There are only two sets of escalators in the entire state of Wyoming, U.S.A.

A ROBOT IN JAPAN OFFICIATED A WEDDING BETWEEN TWO OTHER ROBOTS.

Redheads
in Australia
are sometimes
called
"Blueys."

The **meteorite** that most likely **killed** off the **dinosaurs** was the size of San Francisco, California, U.S.A.

EGYPTOLOGISTS UNEARTHED **2,000-YEAR-OLD** TOMB ART SHOWING A PERSON WALKING A MONGOOSE ON A LEASH.

ZHONGJIANOSAURUS YANGI WAS A DINOSAUR WITH FOUR WINGS, A FEATHERED TAIL, AND STILT-LIKE LEGS.

Humans can **SENSE MORE** than **ONE TRILLION** different smells, a study found.

In the Victorian era, people believed that **TRAIN RIDES** could **CAUSE INSANITY.**

THE WORLD'S FASTEST CAMERA CAN CAPTURE THE MOVEMENT OF LIGHT.

SCIENTISTS THINK LINES ON THE SURFACE OF MARS COULD HAVE BEEN CREATED BY **500-MILE-AN-HOUR** (800-KM/H) **WINDS.**

Scientists developed an **"EXERCISE PILL"** that allowed mice to **RUN ON A TREADMILL** for **70 PERCENT LONGER** than other mice.

A BEACH IN IRELAND DISAPPEARED AND THEN REAPPEARED **33 YEARS LATER.**

The **VENOM** of a brown snake
BECOMES DEADLIER
as the SNAKE GETS OLDER.

A new
SHADE OF BLUE
was **DISCOVERED**
FOR THE FIRST TIME in
200 YEARS.

Scientists invented
SPRAY PAINT
that can turn almost anything
INTO A TOUCH SCREEN.

That's
Weird!

Some **BIRDS**
choose their neighbors
based on
PERSONALITY,
one study found.

Donald Duck's middle name is FAUNTLEROY.

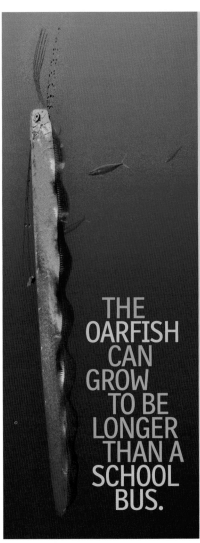

THE OARFISH CAN GROW TO BE LONGER THAN A SCHOOL BUS.

A flawless **pink diamond** was auctioned for **$83 million.**

127

SOME **ZOO** ANIMALS

SNACK ON **"BLOODSICLES"**

TO STAY **COOL** DURING HEAT WAVES.

Choir members' **heartbeats sync** when they **sing,** a study found.

AN
AUSTRIAN
PHOTOGRAPHER
TURNED A
SHIPWRECK
INTO
AN
UNDERWATER ART GALLERY.

A **ZOO** in England banned visitors from wearing **animal print clothes** to avoid confusing the wildlife.

IT TAKES ABOUT THE SAME AMOUNT OF **force** TO PULL YOUR FOOT OUT OF **quicksand** AS IT DOES TO **lift a car.**

Soccer's World Cup trophy is worth about $250,000!

There's a **world snail racing championship** held in England **every year.**

#23

Buttered toast almost always falls butter-side down.

THE LION'S MANE
JELLYFISH
CAN GROW TO
BE LONGER THAN
SEVEN SUVs.

THE CITY OF
AMSTERDAM,
IN THE NETHERLANDS,
HAS MORE **BIKES**
THAN PEOPLE.

CATS AND DOGS CAN GET SUNBURNED.

In **Belgium,** there are postage stamps that smell and taste like chocolate.

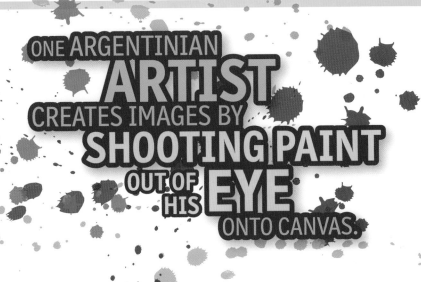

ONE ARGENTINIAN ARTIST CREATES IMAGES BY SHOOTING PAINT OUT OF HIS EYE ONTO CANVAS.

SOME LIZARDS HAVE **GREEN BONES.**

The *Caloplaca obamae* fungus is named after President Obama.

You can cook **fish** in your dishwasher.

A 16-YEAR-OLD **CHEERLEADER** LANDED IN THE RECORD BOOKS AFTER DOING **40 BACK** HANDSPRINGS IN A ROW.

Voyager 1

is the **first spacecraft** to leave the **solar system**— more than **11 billion miles** (17,702,784,000 km) from Earth.

Mistletoe
has no
scent.

420 million years ago, mushrooms grew taller than giraffes.

A MANHATTAN **PIZZERIA** SELLS A **12-INCH** (31-cm) **PIZZA** WITH CAVIAR TOPPING FOR **$1,000.**

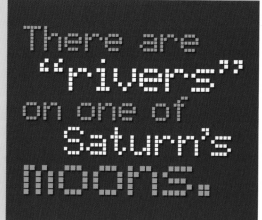

There are "rivers" on one of Saturn's moons.

SOME RATS ARE TRAINED TO SNIFF OUT BOMBS.

You can buy cola-flavored **Cheetos** in Japan.

SNOW ISN'T WHITE; it's translucent.

Parrotfish sleep in a bag of their own mucus.

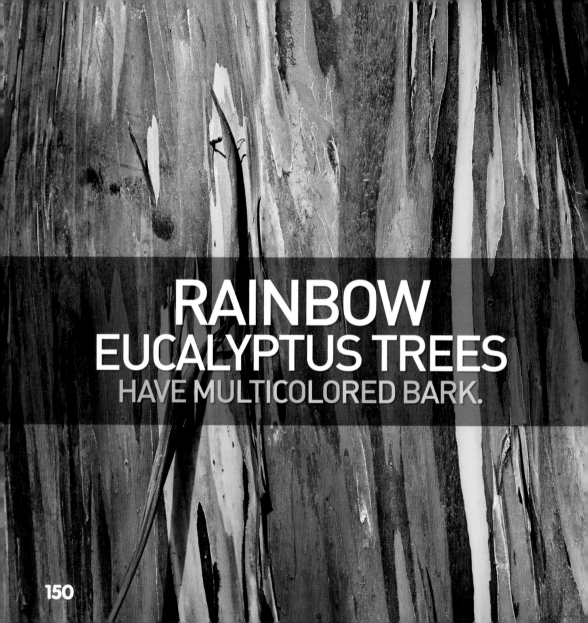

RAINBOW
EUCALYPTUS TREES
HAVE MULTICOLORED BARK.

A tiny park in Oregon, U.S.A., is smaller than a skateboard.

A **WOMAN** IN FLORIDA, U.S.A., FOUND A **STRAWBERRY** SHAPED LIKE A **GRIZZLY BEAR.**

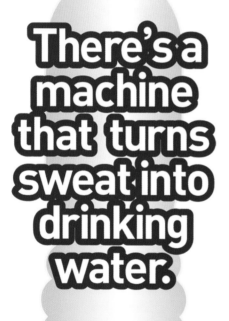

There's a machine that turns sweat into drinking water.

The first Tweet from Google read "I'm 01100110 01100101 01100101 01101100 01101001 01101110 01100111 00100000 01101100 01110101 01100011 01101011 01111001 00001010."

SCOOBY-DOO
WAS ORIGINALLY NAMED
TOO MUCH.

TIGERS AND HOUSE CATS

SHARE 95 PERCENT OF THE SAME GENES.

Northern Spy, Wealthy, and Twenty Ounce are all types of **apples.**

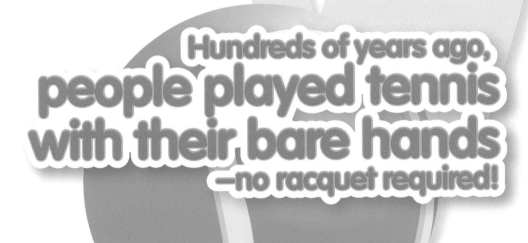

Hundreds of years ago, people played tennis with their bare hands —no racquet required!

King cobras can grow as **long** as a giraffe is tall.

THERE MAY BE **100 TIMES** MORE WATER BENEATH **AFRICA** THAN ON ITS SURFACE.

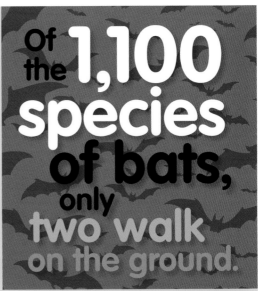

Of the **1,100 species of bats,** only **two walk** on the ground.

AN EXTINCT **VOLCANO** THE SIZE OF **ITALY** LIES UNDERNEATH THE **PACIFIC OCEAN.**

AN OLYMPIC WRESTLING MATCH ONCE LASTED 11 HOURS.

CHIHUAHUA + DACHSHUND

CHIWEENIE

You can mail a postcard from **AUSTRALIA'S** Great Barrier Reef—45 miles from shore.

(72 km)

SOME **FISH** CAN **GROW** ALMOST A **QUARTER OF THEIR BODY LENGTH** IN A SINGLE DAY.

Earth bulges at the Equator.

PEOPLE WHO LOVE TO READ TEND TO BE **NICER** AND **MORE UNDERSTANDING,** ONE STUDY FOUND.

AN INTERNET CHEF COOKS TINY FOOD—from doughnuts the size of Cheerios to apple pies the size of silver dollars—in a tiny **KITCHEN THE SIZE OF A BRIEFCASE.**

AT JAIL CAFÉ, a Los Angeles theme restaurant from the 1920s, waiters dressed as convicts served diners who sat in fake **PRISON CELLS.**

TO ESCAPE EARTH'S GRAVITY, A ROCKET HAS TO BE **TRAVELING** ABOUT SEVEN MILES A SECOND (11 KM/S)—25,000 MILES AN HOUR (40,235 KM/H)!

SNAKES IN CUBA HUNT IN GROUPS BY **HANGING IN CAVE ENTRANCES** AND WAITING **FOR BATS.**

A 115-YEAR-OLD FOSSILIZED MUSHROOM was uncovered in **NORTHEAST BRAZIL.**

ONE DINOSAUR MADE A NEST THE SIZE OF A **MONSTER TRUCK TIRE.**

WHEN A **FEMALE DRAGONFLY** IS ANNOYED BY A MALE, SHE WILL **PLAY DEAD** UNTIL HE LEAVES.

THERE IS A **3.3-FOOT** (1-M)-TALL **LEGO MODEL** OF THE **SATURN V ROCKET** THAT LAUNCHED ASTRONAUTS TO THE MOON.

A San Francisco, California, U.S.A., company **3-D PRINTED A HOUSE IN 24 HOURS.**

A **3,000-YEAR-OLD WHITE HORSE** the **SIZE OF A FOOTBALL FIELD** is carved into a British hillside.

DUBAI,
a city in the United Arab Emirates, has the
WORLD'S FIRST ROBOT POLICE OFFICER.

That's Weird!

It would take the strength of **five people to** "*tip*" a standing cow.

HELLO
my name is

THE BIRD ON THE TWITTER LOGO IS NAMED LARRY.

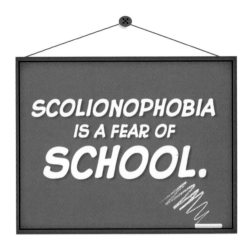

SCOLIONOPHOBIA IS A FEAR OF SCHOOL.

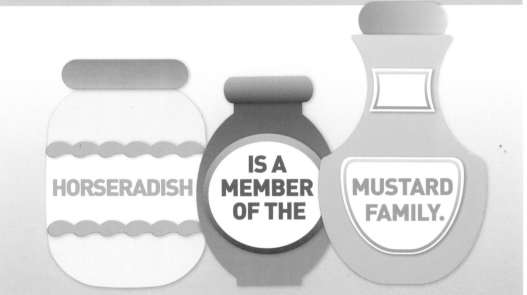

HORSERADISH IS A MEMBER OF THE MUSTARD FAMILY.

SEVERAL SHIPS
ARE BURIED

UNDER BUILDINGS

IN SAN FRANCISCO, CALIFORNIA, U.S.A.

PEOPLE WAITED IN A 7-MILE (11-km) LINE TO EAT AT THE FIRST EVER MCDONALD'S IN KUWAIT.

Alaska is the **northernmost, westernmost, and easternmost state** in the United States.

AVOCADOS ARE TOXIC TO MOST BIRDS.

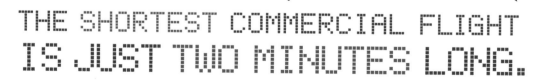

THE SHORTEST COMMERCIAL FLIGHT IS JUST TWO MINUTES LONG.

"Watermelon snow"

IS TINTED PINK AND SMELLS SWEET.

SOME **BUTTERFLIES** DRINK TURTLE TEARS.

AMERICANS BUY SOME **THREE MILLION MILES** (4,828,032 km) OF DENTAL FLOSS EVERY YEAR.

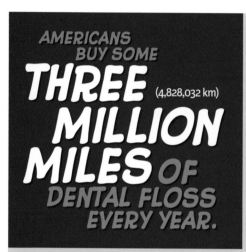

Vinegar can dissolve pearls.

DON'T TRY THIS AT HOME!

WHEN THREATENED, THE HELLBENDER SALAMANDER, ALSO CALLED A SNOT OTTER, OOZES CLEAR SLIME.

Gorillas sleep in **nests.**

You spend about an hour a day CHEWING.

ALL **CLOWNFISH** ARE BORN **MALE.**

Lobsters, seals, and swans may have been on the Pilgrims' Thanksgiving menu.

Newborn babies don't produce **tears** when they **CRY.**

THE **EYE** OF A HURRICANE ON **SATURN** IS SO HUGE, IT WOULD **STRETCH** FROM **LONDON,** ENGLAND, TO MOSCOW, **RUSSIA.**

179

Thousands of brand-new **sneakers** once washed ashore on a Dutch island.

Some astronauts
train for space walks
by walking on the
OCEAN FLOOR.

Giant **CLAMS** can grow AS LONG AS **two** skateboards.

Kiwifruits were originally called "melonettes."

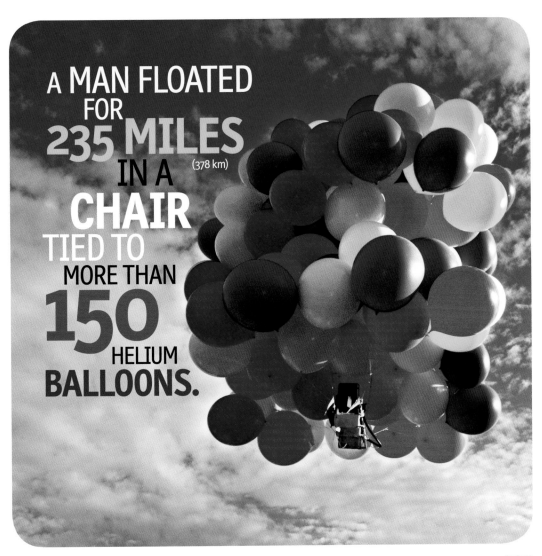

A MAN FLOATED FOR **235 MILES** (378 km) IN A **CHAIR** TIED TO MORE THAN **150** HELIUM **BALLOONS.**

THE SOUND OF AN **ICEBERG BREAKING** IS LOUDER THAN **214 OIL TANKER ENGINES.**

A
FISHERMAN
NEAR
NORWAY
REELED IN A
9-FOOT-
LONG (2.7-m)
HALIBUT
THAT
WEIGHED
MORE THAN A
GORILLA.

It is a crime to wear jeans in North Korea.

MORE THAN
30 MILLION PEOPLE
IN CHINA
LIVE IN CAVES.

PIGEONS
CAN RECOGNIZE
THEMSELVES
IN A MIRROR.

An **alligator** loses and regrows **teeth** up to **50** times during its lifetime.

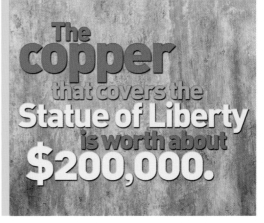

The **copper** that covers the **Statue of Liberty** is worth about **$200,000.**

A whale's EARWAX can be as thick as a mattress.

You can **stay** IN A **luxury** cave at an **inn** in NEW MEXICO, U.S.A.

SCIENTISTS THINK THAT IT RAINS GLASS ON SOME PLANETS.

THERE ARE **NO SEAGULLS** IN HAWAII, U.S.A.

ASH FROM VOLCANIC ERUPTIONS CAN MAKE THE **MOON** LOOK BLUE FROM EARTH.

A species of snub-nosed **monkey** *sneezes.*

EIGHT COLLEGE FOOTBALL PLAYERS COMPETED AGAINST TWO ASIAN ELEPHANTS IN A WATERMELON-EATING CONTEST.

(THE HUMANS LOST.)

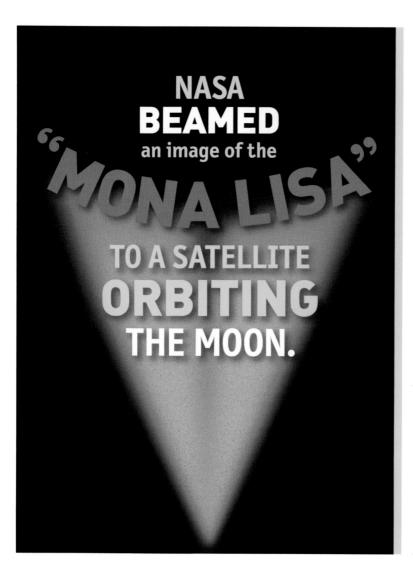

NASA
BEAMED
an image of the
"**MONA LISA**"
TO A SATELLITE
ORBITING
THE MOON.

PREHISTORIC PEOPLE USED "**SUPERGLUE**" MADE FROM TREE SAP AND PIGMENT SOME 70,000 YEARS AGO.

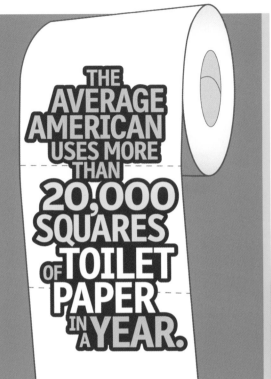

THE AVERAGE AMERICAN USES MORE THAN 20,000 SQUARES OF TOILET PAPER IN A YEAR.

THERE ARE UP TO 500 DIMPLES ON EVERY GOLF BALL.

THE THINNEST GLASS IN THE WORLD IS TWO ATOMS THICK.

Horseshoe crabs have powder blue blood.

Some **pigs** have **curly hair.**

An **ASTRONAUT** once hosted a **RADIO SHOW** from space.

SOME **MOTH COCOONS** CAN BE USED TO MAKE PURSES.

SOME **FISH** CAN **TASTE** WITH THEIR TAILS.

The scientific name for **brain freeze** is *sphenopalatine ganglioneuralgia.*

CHIPMUNKS **see** in *slow motion.*

197

Tyrannosaurus **rex** could probably **swim.**

THERE'S A **HOTEL** WITH **GUEST ROOMS** MADE OUT OF OLD **DRAINAGE PIPES.**

january   february   march   april

may   **Large crocodiles can survive for more than a year without eating.**   august

cember

THERE ARE
MORE THAN

1,900
EDIBLE
INSECT SPECIES
ON EARTH.

THERE'S A **BAND** THAT **PLAYS** INSTRUMENTS MADE FROM OLD **CAR PARTS.**

THE "STRUTBONE" IS MADE FROM THE STRUTS OF A CAR!

ATHLETES ATE CHEESECAKE DURING THE FIRST OLYMPIC GAMES IN GREECE.

Flying vampire frogs have black fangs when they are tadpoles.

The ancient Greeks used sheep sweat to make lipstick.

YOU HAVE ABOUT **FOUR MILLION** SWEAT GLANDS IN YOUR BODY.

There's a
pink lake
in Australia.

THERE IS A **WETSUIT**

DESIGNED **TO CONFUSE SHARKS.**

Scientists think **sharks** are color-blind.

GUESS WHAT?

Chew this if you're in a bad mood!
WHAT?

Some frogs are way greener than they appear
WHY?

The speedy cheetah is slower than a teeny bug!
HOW?

WANNA FIND OUT?

The FUN doesn't have to end here! Find these far-out facts and more in *Weird But True! 7.*

FACTFINDER

Boldface indicates illustrations.

FACTFINDER

FACTFINDER

FACTFINDER

PHOTO CREDITS

For more information, visit nationalgeographic
.com, call 1-800-647-5463, or write to the
following address:

National Geographic Partners
1145 17th Street N.W.
Washington, D.C. 20036-4688 U.S.A.

Visit us online at
nationalgeographic.com/books

For librarians and teachers:
ngchildrensbooks.org

More for kids from National Geographic:
natgeokids.com

For information about special discounts
for bulk purchases, please contact National
Geographic Books Special Sales:
specialsales@natgeo.com

For rights or permissions inquiries, please
contact National Geographic Books Subsidiary
Rights: bookrights@natgeo.com

Designed by Rachael Hamm Plett, Moduza Design

First edition published 2014
Reissued and updated 2018

Trade paperback: 978-1-4263-3114-5
Reinforced library binding ISBN:
978-1-4263-3115-2

The publisher would like to thank Jen Agresta,
project manager; Julie Beer, researcher;
Michelle Harris, researcher; Stephanie
Drimmer, researcher; Robin Terry, project
editor; Ariane Szu-Tu, project editor; Paige
Towler, project editor; Eva Absher-Schantz, art
director; Julide Dengel, art director; Kathryn
Robbins, art director; Ruthie Thompson,
designer; Lori Epstein, photo director; Hillary
Leo, photo editor; Alix Inchausti, production
editor; and Anne LeongSon and Gus Tello,
production assistants.

Printed in China
18/PPS/1